THE EVOLUTION

OF AFRICA'S MAJOR NATIONS

Ethiopia

THE EVOLUTION
OF AFRICA'S MAJOR NATIONS

Ethiopia

Jim Corrigan

MC Mason Crest
Philadelphia

Mason Crest
370 Reed Road
Broomall, PA 19008
www.masoncrest.com

Copyright © 2013 by Mason Crest, an imprint of National Highlights, Inc. All rights reserved.
Printed and bound in the Hashemite Kingdom of Jordan.

CPSIA Compliance Information: Batch #EAMN2013-10. For further information,
contact Mason Crest at 1-866-MCP-Book.

First printing

1 3 5 7 9 8 6 4 2

Library of Congress Cataloging-in-Publication Data

Corrigan, Jim.
    Ethiopia / Jim Corrigan.
        p. cm. — (The evolution of Africa's major nations.)
    Includes bibliographical references and index.
    ISBN 978-1-4222-2179-2 (hardcover)
    ISBN 978-1-4222-2207-2 (pbk.)
    ISBN 978-1-4222-9420-8 (ebook)
    1. Ethiopia—Juvenile literature. I. Title. II. Series: Evolution of Africa's major nations.
    DT373.C672 2011
    963—dc22
                            2010048007

Table of Contents

Africa: Progress, Problems, and Promise

Robert I. Rotberg

Africa is the cradle of humankind, but for millennia it was off the familiar, beaten path of global commerce and discovery. Its many peoples therefore developed largely apart from the diffusion of modern knowledge and the spread of technological innovation until the 17th through 19th centuries. With the coming to Africa of the book, the wheel, the hoe, and the modern rifle and cannon, foreigners also brought the vastly destructive transatlantic slave trade, oppression, discrimination, and onerous colonial rule. Emerging from that crucible of European rule, Africans created nationalistic movements and then claimed their numerous national independences in the 1960s. The result is the world's largest continental assembly of new countries.

There are 53 members of the African Union, a regional political grouping, and 48 of those nations lie south of the Sahara. Fifteen of them, including mighty Ethiopia, are landlocked, making international trade and economic growth that much more arduous and expensive. Access to navigable rivers is limited, natural harbors are few, soils are poor and thin, several countries largely consist of miles and miles of sand, and tropical diseases have sapped the strength and productivity of innumerable millions. Being landlocked, having few resources (although countries along Africa's west coast have tapped into deep offshore petroleum and gas reservoirs), and being beset by malaria, tuberculosis, schistosomiasis, AIDS, and many other maladies has kept much of Africa poor for centuries.

Thirty-two of the world's poorest 44 countries are African. Hunger is common. So is rapid deforestation and desertification. Unemployment rates are often over 50 percent, for jobs are few—even in agriculture. Where Africa once was a land of small villages and a few large cities, with almost everyone engaged in growing grain or root crops or grazing cattle, camels, sheep, and goats, today more than half of all the more than 1 billion Africans, especially those who live south of the Sahara, reside in towns and cities. Traditional agriculture hardly pays, and a number of countries in Africa—particularly the smaller and more fragile ones—can no longer feed themselves.

There is not one Africa, for the continent is full of contradictions and variety. Of the 750 million people living south of the Sahara, at least 150 million live in Nigeria, 85 million in Ethiopia, 68 million in the Democratic Republic of the Congo, and 49 million in South Africa. By contrast, tiny Djibouti and Equatorial Guinea have fewer than 1 million people each, and prosperous Botswana and Namibia each are under 2.2 million in population. Within some countries, even medium-sized ones like Zambia (12 million), there are a plethora of distinct ethnic groups speaking separate languages. Zambia, typical with its multitude of competing entities, has 70 such peoples, roughly broken down into four language and cultural zones. Three of those languages jostle with English for primacy.

Primary school children in class in Harar, Ethiopia.

The baboon-like Gelada is a species unique to the Ethiopian highlands.

Given the kaleidoscopic quality of African culture and deep-grained poverty, it is no wonder that Africa has developed economically and politically less rapidly than other regions. Since independence from colonial rule, weak governance has also plagued Africa and contributed significantly to the widespread poverty of its peoples. Only Botswana and offshore Mauritius have been governed democratically without interruption since independence. Both are among Africa's wealthiest countries, too, thanks to the steady application of good governance.

Aside from those two nations, and South Africa, Africa has been a continent of coups since 1960, with massive and oil-rich Nigeria suffering incessant periods of harsh, corrupt, autocratic military rule. Nearly every other country on or around the continent, small and large, has been plagued by similar bouts of instability and dictatorial rule. In the 1970s and 1980s Idi Amin ruled Uganda capriciously and Jean-Bedel Bokassa proclaimed himself emperor of the Central African Republic. Macias Nguema of Equatorial Guinea was another in that same mold. More recently Daniel arap Moi held Kenya in thrall and Robert Mugabe has imposed himself on once-prosperous Zimbabwe. In both of those cases, as in the case of Gnassingbe Eyadema in Togo and the late Mobutu Sese Seko in Congo, these presidents stole wildly and drove entire peoples and their nations into penury. Corruption is common in Africa, and so are a weak rule-of-law framework, misplaced development, high expenditures on soldiers and low expenditures on health and education, and a widespread (but not universal) refusal on the part of leaders to work well for their followers and citizens.

Conflict between groups within countries has also been common in Africa. More than 12 million Africans have been killed in civil wars since 1990, while another 9 million have become refugees. Decades of conflict in Sudan led to a January 2011 referendum in which the people of southern Sudan voted overwhelmingly to secede and form a new state. In early 2011, anti-government protests spread throughout North Africa, ultimately toppling long-standing regimes in Tunisia and Egypt. That same year, there were serious ongoing hostilities within Chad, Ivory Coast, Libya, the Niger Delta region of Nigeria, and Somalia.

Despite such dangers, despotism, and decay, Africa is improving. Botswana and Mauritius, now joined by South Africa, Senegal, Kenya, and Ghana, are beacons of democratic growth and enlightened rule. Uganda and Senegal are taking the lead in combating and reducing the spread of AIDS, and others are following. There are serious signs of the kinds of progressive economic policy changes that might lead to prosperity for more of Africa's peoples. The trajectory in Africa is positive.

A common misconception about Ethiopia is that it is a dry, desert-like wasteland. (Opposite) A hiker enjoys a view in the Simien Mountains, a beautiful example of some of Ethiopia's more scenic areas of land. (Right) Blue Nile Falls is a popular tourist attraction. In Amharic, a language of Ethiopia, they are known as Tis Abay ("smoking water").

Misunderstood Nation

ETHIOPIA HAS BECOME synonymous with desert wasteland and starving refugees. When asked about this East African nation, most people recall television news reports of endless drought and despair. Images such as these make a lasting impression, but they do not accurately reflect the country as a whole.

The image of Ethiopia that is presented to most of the world is distorted. It is not a vast wasteland, but rather contains some of the most beautiful scenery in the world. Drought does not plague the entire country, but is primarily confined to the northern regions.

There are other misconceptions about Ethiopia. For example, it is not a land of primitive nomadic tribes, as many have heard. Civilizations are known to have thrived in the area since the time of the ancient Egyptians and perhaps even earlier. During the age of imperialism, a line of strong Ethiopian emperors defended the country from foreign rule while the rest of East Africa and other regions were being colonized. Because it avoided colonization for so long, Ethiopia is considered the oldest independent nation in Africa.

The country's extensive history and proximity to the Middle East are primary factors behind the great diversity of its people today. There are nine major ethnic groups and a number of smaller but distinctly different minorities. A total of 83 languages, and more than 200 dialects, are spoken by these various groups.

ENVIRONMENT

Situated in the Horn of Africa, Ethiopia is a large country that occupies an area nearly twice the size of Texas. Surrounded by Eritrea and Djibouti in the north, Sudan in the west, Kenya in the south, and Somalia in the east, the country is entirely *landlocked*. The capital city, Addis Ababa, is located in the center.

Forty million years ago, volcanic activity added soaring mountains to the flat, featureless East African plain. Nowhere was this activity more pronounced than in Ethiopia's interior, which was transformed into a massive *plateau*. This central highland rises sharply to an average height of 5,500 feet (1,680 meters) and towers above the low-lying desert that surrounds it on three sides. To the south, the plateau gradually descends into Lake Turkana and Kenya.

Jagged peaks and deep valleys scar the Ethiopian highlands. The Great Rift Valley, a 3,000-mile-long (4,828-km) depression traversing East Africa,

THE GEOGRAPHY OF ETHIOPIA

Location: Eastern Africa, west of Somalia

Area: (slightly more than one-fifth the size of the U.S.)
  total: 426,373 square miles (1,104,300 sq km)
  land: 386,102 square miles (1,000,000 sq km)
  water: 40,270 square miles (104,300 sq km)

Borders: Djibouti, 217 miles (349 km); Eritrea, 567 miles (912 km); Kenya, 535 miles (861 km); Somalia, 994 miles (1,600 km); Sudan, 998 miles (1,606 km)

Climate: tropical monsoon with wide topographic-induced variation

Terrain: high plateau with central mountain range divided by Great Rift Valley

Elevation extremes:
  lowest point: Danakil Depression, 410 feet (125 meters) below sea level
  highest point: Ras Dejen, 14,872 feet (4,533 meters)

Natural hazards: geologically active Great Rift Valley susceptible to earthquakes, volcanic eruptions; frequent droughts

Source: CIA World Factbook, 2011.

passes through the highlands in a southwesterly direction. Ras Dejen is the highest of the plateau's 20 major peaks, at 15,158 feet (4,620 meters). It is also the fourth-highest peak in Africa and part of an extensive mountain range, known as the Simiens, in the northern region.

Several species of animals living in the Simiens are not found anywhere else on the globe. The Simien wolf is the most rare canine species in the world. Known to Ethiopians as *ky kebero* (red jackal), it roams the grasslands hunting for rodents. Although the species was once prolific, there are now believed to be fewer than 600 Simien wolves left in the world.

A long-horned mountain goat called the *walia ibex* is even more endangered, largely as a result of overhunting. The roughly 300 walia ibexes remaining on the steep mountain shelves of the Simiens are protected, but it is undetermined whether the species will ever recover. Ethiopian wildlife officials hope that the walia ibex will follow the same course as the mountain nyala, a rare type of antelope indigenous only to southern Ethiopia. Once on the verge of extinction in the late 1980s, the mountain nyala population has rebounded to about 3,000.

Salt mountains in the Danakil desert. Centuries ago, this area of the desert used to be a salt lake, and so there are large deposits of salt beneath the sand.

Ethiopia does not possess the abundance of wildlife found in other African nations such as Kenya and South Africa, but its habitats are home to a few unique species. Geladas are baboon-like monkeys found throughout northern Ethiopia. They live in troops of 500 or more individuals. The gelada is also known as the "bleeding heart baboon" because of a red heart-shaped patch on its chest. Birds are also plentiful with over 800 species, 16 of which are exclusively found in Ethiopia. A wide variety of predators and prey animals live in the country's nine national parks and many reserves.

Four major river systems flow from the Ethiopian highlands: the Blue Nile, the White Nile, the Baro, and the Tekeze. The Blue Nile flows southward from Lake Tana, Ethiopia's largest body of water. It then turns northwest through Sudan and into Egypt's Nile River, where it provides two-thirds of that river's water. The Blue Nile, Ethiopia's largest river, has been traversing this route for eons. As a result, it has carved an enormous gorge in northwestern Ethiopia that is similar to the Grand Canyon in the United States.

Ethiopia has many lakes, and several fill the craters of extinct volcanoes. With volcanic activity and earthquakes still relatively common in the Great Rift Valley, some of the country's volcanoes are still active.

CLIMATE AND FAMINE

Ethiopia's highland valleys and ravines are thick with jungle vegetation, while the slopes and meadows are covered with grasses. Several of the highest peaks are occasionally covered with snow.

The average highland temperature ranges from 61°F (16°C) to 72°F (22°C). The annual rainfall varies between 50 inches (127 centimeters) and 70 inches

Ethiopian children play in the water of a well in Jedane. The 302-foot-deep well, drilled by U.S. Navy Seebees, provides clean water to more than 3,400 area residents and their livestock.

(178 cm), depending on elevation. In contrast, the lowlands surrounding the plateau are hot and arid with sparse desert vegetation, the average temperature is 80°F (27°C), and the annual rainfall is only about 20 inches (51 cm).

Ethiopia's driest region is the Danakil Desert, located along the border with Eritrea and Djibouti. Daytime temperatures there routinely reach 120°F (50°C), making it one of the hottest places in the world. The Danakil Desert also contains a large depression that is one of the lowest points on the earth's surface. There a gigantic salt lake once existed, and for centuries Ethiopians have mined salt from this lakebed. The salt is carved out in bricks called *amoles* and transported by camel to the highlands, where it is in great demand.

Ethiopia's rainy season lasts from June through September and is followed by a long dry season. A second, shorter rainy season may occur in February or March. Ethiopia's rainfall tends to come in heavy cloudbursts that arrive and pass relatively quickly.

So why are the northern highlands so prone to famine? At least part of the answer has to do with Ethiopia's location. Regions bordering a desert are susceptible to erratic rainfall patterns. This is particularly true between the latitudes of 15 and 20 degrees. Within this zone, the hot, dry winds of the desert have been known to encroach on adjacent areas and cause severe drought. Ethiopia's northern highlands flank the extremely arid Danakil Desert and fall within the high-risk zone that scientists have identified. In recent decades, some scientists have concluded that human activity is also responsible for Ethiopian droughts. They point to environmental damage, such as widespread pollution and deforestation, which can worsen drought cycles.

The water shortages have an immediate and devastating impact on Ethiopia's food supply. Only 10 percent of the land is truly *arable*, or suitable for farming. Further, Ethiopian farmers use outdated methods that often limit them to growing only enough food to feed their families. With little or no food reserves, a drought-induced crop failure leads to near-instant famine. A violent conflict can make a famine even worse because international aid organizations will have trouble safely reaching affected regions.

(Opposite) The Ezana stela, the largest single piece of stone ever lifted by human beings, sits in the heart of Aksum, overlooking the town. (Right) Children play on a destroyed tank near Dese, in the northern part of the country. Ethiopia was torn apart by civil war between 1974 and 1991.

2 A Long and Turbulent History

THE FIRST HUMAN inhabitants of Ethiopia settled in the northern highlands. Prehistoric cave paintings suggest the presence of hunter-gatherer societies there as early as the Stone Age.

By about 3000 B.C., these groups were learning to farm and make pottery. The ancient Egyptians also visited the region during this time. The Egyptians and Greeks referred to Ethiopia and the surrounding area as Punt. During the time of Christ and perhaps earlier, Egyptian and Greek merchants sailed down the Red Sea to trade for gold and ivory with the peoples they encountered.

EARLY EMPIRES

By the first century A.D., Ethiopia's first major kingdom had risen. Known as the Aksum Empire, it was based in the present-day country's far north and

Christianity in Ethiopia dates to the fourth century A.D. The Church of St. George at Lalibela was carved from solid rock in the early 13th century. From above, the church looks like a cross.

was an important trade center. Traders came from India, Rome, and the Middle East to exchange goods in Aksum. The people of the empire had their own written language, called *Ge'ez*, and they quickly embraced Christianity when believers brought it from the Holy Land in the fourth century.

Aksum's influential status only lasted a few hundred years. By 750, the Middle East's center of trade had shifted from the Red Sea to the Persian Gulf and Indian Ocean. The empire declined and eventually withered. While tribes within the empire clashed, the region slipped away from the world's attention and out of historical account.

Ethiopia emerged from its dark age in the year 1270, when a ruler named Yekuno Amlak came to power. He claimed to be a direct descendant of ancient Israel's legendary King Solomon. The claim was significant to the people because Ethiopian lore had already identified King Solomon, who ruled Israel from 961 to 922 B.C., as an important and powerful ally. From 1270 onward, Ethiopian emperors would claim to be Solomonic descendants.

For several centuries, the states of the Ethiopian region enjoyed relative peace and prosperity. Literature and religious art became common, and stone churches were built as Christianity continued to spread through the highlands. In the surrounding desert regions, Islam was gaining popularity. The first Muslim settlers arrived in Ethiopia in A.D. 615, during the lifetime of the prophet Muhammad. Muslims continued migrating to eastern Ethiopia for centuries afterward. Two distinct cultures evolved: the Christian kingdom of the highlands and the Islamic population of the lowlands.

The two groups tolerated one another's presence for an extended period, but tensions gradually developed. Occasional skirmishes turned into open warfare in the early 1500s, when the Muslims launched a series of attacks. The Christians contacted Portugal, a European power with troops stationed in the area, and requested assistance in fighting off the assaults. Portugal obliged and in 1543 the Muslims were defeated in a fierce battle near Lake Tana. Hostilities continued for nearly two decades, until finally neither side had the stamina to fight any longer. A period of tense peace followed the conflict.

Over the next 300 years, a string of weak emperors allowed the Christian empire to slowly disintegrate. By the 1850s, Ethiopian society consisted only of small, disorganized territories. Meanwhile, Egyptians had realized that the source of the Blue Nile River, Lake Tana, lay in a abundant region and they sought to possess the northern highlands. With much difficulty, the Ethiopians of the western territories fought off Egyptian raids.

Kasa Hayla was a leader of one of these western territories. Upon realizing that Ethiopia needed to be unified if it wished to remain independent from foreign rule, he organized a national army and crowned himself

Emperor Theodore II. As emperor, Theodore worked to eliminate some of the inequities of Ethiopian life. He outlawed the slave trade and seized church-owned land, redistributing it to peasant farmers.

While popular with the common man, these measures angered the country's priests and noblemen. Theodore's power declined and amid rebellion he sought assistance from Britain, who only ignored him. In desperation, Theodore responded by holding several visiting British officials as prisoners, hoping to spur the government into action. But the plan backfired, and instead of rushing to Theodore's aid as the emperor had imagined, Britain dispatched 32,000 troops to capture him.

DEALING WITH THE EUROPEANS

Theodore was unprepared for the invasion of British forces. He and his soldiers were quickly encircled, and rather than be taken prisoner, Theodore committed suicide in 1869. The emperor who had labored for an independent and unified Ethiopia lay dead after inadvertently drawing a major European power into his country's affairs.

Britain ultimately proved to have little interest in Ethiopia. Other African regions, such as modern-day Kenya and Uganda, had greater natural resources and thus would fare better as colonies. Britain was satisfied with just running the Ethiopian trading port of Massawa (now located in Eritrea). In 1885, the British signed an agreement that gave the port to Italy, which was far more eager to colonize Ethiopia.

In the 1880s a number of skirmishes took place between Italian and Ethiopian forces. In 1889, newly crowned Emperor Menelik II (1844–1913) signed the Treaty of Uccialli. Instead of bringing peace, the treaty only led to more fighting. The disagreement largely resulted from the Italian leaders' devious tactics, because while the Amharic version of the treaty stated that Ethiopians were only giving up modern-day Eritrea, the Italian version of the treaty stated that Italy now possessed the entire territory. Shortly after Menelik realized he was the victim of a hoax, he led Ethiopia into full-scale war.

The conflict between the two states dragged on for several years. It ended in 1896, when Ethiopian soldiers brutally defeated the Italians at the Battle of Adwa in the north. The Italians withdrew to Eritrea, marking the first time an African army could claim victory over European forces. The Battle of Adwa is still considered one of the most legendary events in Ethiopian history.

While neighboring territories were being carved up into European colonies during this period, Ethiopia remained stubbornly independent. During the first decades of the 20th century, Ethiopia evolved into the unified state that Emperor Theodore had once so desperately wanted. Emperor Haile Selassie, who was crowned in 1930, drafted a constitution and established a parliament. Although most power remained with the throne, the emperor had demonstrated more tolerance than his predecessors, as the country moved toward a more modern form of government.

However, war clouds soon gathered over Ethiopia once again. Remembering its defeat at Adwa, Italy sought revenge in 1935. Italian troops crossed the border from Eritrea in October and pushed the unprepared Ethiopians aside. By May 1936, the entire country was occupied.

The Italian occupation was brief but harsh, and Ethiopians suffered

For decades Italy sought to colonize Ethiopia. In 1935, Emperor Haile Selassie (on horseback) tried to defend the country against an Italian invasion, but his poorly equipped and inexperienced army was no match for the highly trained and well-armed Italian troops. The Italian occupation of Ethiopia lasted from 1936 until 1941.

under the oppressive rule. Italy at this time was a member of the Axis powers, the alliance of nations responsible for starting World War II. British forces, fighting in Africa against the Axis powers, liberated Ethiopia in January 1941, paving the way for Haile Selassie to reclaim the throne.

At the conclusion of World War II, Haile Selassie requested that Eritrea be returned to Ethiopia. He argued that Italy had taken the land unfairly over

50 years earlier. The United Nations agreed, and, without consulting Eritrea, placed the country under Ethiopian control. This decision led to a dispute between Ethiopians and Eritreans that would last for decades.

MODERN ETHIOPIA

Haile Selassie remained emperor throughout the 1950s and 1960s, but did little to improve the lives of his subjects or the economy. Wealthy landowners exploited peasant farmers. The country, lacking even the most basic *infrastructure*, became one of the poorest nations in the world. Haile Selassie worried only about maintaining his grip on power and dabbling in world politics. A military coup attempt was organized in 1960, though it was crushed and its ringleaders were killed.

During the next 13 years, revolts broke out in various regions of the country. Student demonstrations and street violence became common, and several local governments were overthrown. The people of Eritrea also demanded independence during this period. When the emperor refused, the Eritreans began organizing into rebel armies. The Ethiopian army became divided over its loyalties to the emperor and to the people.

The country reached a new low in 1973, when famine struck in the north and roughly 200,000 people died. Finally, the military decided that Haile Selassie's rule could continue no longer. The emperor was removed from power and placed under arrest on September 12, 1974. He was murdered shortly afterwards.

A committee of military leaders was established to run Ethiopia. The group was known as the Derg, and Colonel Mengistu Haile Mariam was its

After Haile Selassie was removed from power, Colonel Mengistu Haile Mariam gained control of Ethiopia. Mengistu was a socialist leader and his reign was marked by famine and violence. He encouraged attacks on people suspected of opposing his government, and hundreds of thousands of Ethiopians were arrested or killed.

chairman. Mengistu did not tolerate dissent, and he executed his opponents, including several members of the Derg. Three years after Haile Selassie's overthrow, Mengistu became dictator of Ethiopia.

Mengistu thought *socialism* was the answer to his country's problems. His government seized all of Ethiopia's farmland and tried to manage agricultural production. But his programs failed and in 1979, another famine swept across the north. At least 10,000 people starved to death.

Government opposition groups secretly sprung up and began staging guerilla attacks in Ethiopian cities. Mengistu responded by providing weapons to anyone still considered loyal to his government, including untrained civilians. They were told to shoot anyone suspected of being disloyal. During this horrifying period, called the Red Terror, over 100,000 people suddenly disappeared.

The second half of the 1980s marked perhaps the most tumultuous period in Ethiopian history. A drought in 1984 resulted in one of the world's worst famines. The country was ravaged, and roughly one million people died. Many international observes blamed a share of the casualties on the government, which withheld donated food shipments as a way to wield political power.

Famine-stricken people wait for the distribution of food in Tulu Awlia, North Ethiopia. The famine in Ethiopia during the mid-1980s was one of the worst in history, resulting in the deaths of approximately one million people.

A member of the Eritrean People's Liberation Front (EPLF) aims a rifle, 1988. The EPLF fought for 27 years to obtain Eritrean independence from Ethiopia, which finally occurred in 1993.

During the years of the famine, Eritrean liberation forces, organized as the Eritrean People's Liberation Front (EPLF), captured large swaths of land. The EPLF was a well-trained army that continued to score victories against the Ethiopian army, steadily advancing from the countryside to the major cities of Eritrea, including the port of Massawa in 1990, and the capital, Asmara, a year later. Two years after this victory, the Eritreans were presented with a referendum, and they voted for independence.

Around this same time Ethiopian anti-government groups, formed as the Ethiopian People's Revolutionary Democratic Front (EPRDF), were scoring major victories against the government's army. Mengistu's attempts to hold peace talks with the EPRDF were too late, and in May 1991, the rebels fought their way into the capital city of Addis Ababa. Mengistu then boarded a plane and fled to Zimbabwe.

The new government that emerged was committed to democracy. Elections were held to select representatives, a new constitution was drawn up, and Meles Zenawi was elected Ethiopia's prime minister. Charges of war crimes were brought against Mengistu and 5,000 of his supporters, but to date, the government has been unable to extradite the former dictator from Zimbabwe.

Ever since Ethiopia recognized Eritrea's independence in 1993, the two nations have squabbled over their shared border. The disagreement escalated into open warfare in 1998 with a series of ferocious battles that failed to resolve the dispute. Estimates of casualties on both sides ranged from 70,000 to 100,000 people.

Ethiopia's international reputation has suffered as a result of the border dispute. As part of the peace treaty in 2000, both sides agreed to abide by the ruling of an international border commission. The ruling, handed down in 2002, found in favor of Eritrea, yet Ethiopia challenged the decision, arguing that it was arrived at unfairly. As a result, the dispute remains unresolved. Both nations claim that they will not start another war, but their armies stand poised and tensions run high. Unable to complete its mission, the United Nations formally withdrew its peacekeeping forces in July of 2008.

More recently, a rebel force calling itself the Ogaden National Liberation Front has waged several violent uprisings against the government. The situation only worsened in 2010 after highly contested elections awarded the EPRDF and Prime Minister Meles Zenawi a fourth term.

(Opposite) A view of the Ethiopian Parliament building, the meeting place of the House of Federation and the House of People's Representatives. (Right) Meles Zenawi has served as Ethiopia's prime minister since 1995.

3 A Young Democracy

ETHIOPIA IS A FEDERAL republic, which means that a central government of elected representatives tends to national affairs while individual state governments handle regional issues. Ethiopia contains nine states and two city-states (Addis Ababa and Dire Dawa). Each state is divided into local districts, called *woredas*. Boundaries for states, and for some *woredas*, are based on ethnic lines. In other words, each state is primarily composed of one ethnic group (with the exception of the state of Southern Nations, Nationalities and Peoples, which is made up of 45 different ethnic groups).

GOVERNMENT INSTITUTIONS

The national government has an executive branch with both a president and a prime minister. However, the actual power rests with the prime minister, as the president's role is largely ceremonial. The president is elected by the legislature and may not serve more than two six-year terms.

The political party that holds the most power in the legislature following each election appoints the prime minister. The prime minister chooses his or her cabinet, known as the Council of Ministers. These advisors head important government agencies such as the Ministry of Health and the Ministry of

A 2011 meeting of the African Union in Addis Ababa. Ethiopia is an important member of this organization, which was formed to help the states of Africa work together diplomatically and economically.

Agriculture. Meles Zenawi, a leader in the rebel movement that overthrew Mengistu and the Derg, has been the prime minister since 1995.

The legislature, known as Parliament, consists of two chambers. The upper chamber is the House of Federation and the lower chamber is the House of People's Representatives. The 108 members of the House of Federation serve five-year terms and are designated by state officials. The 548 members of the House of People's Representatives also serve five-year terms, though Ethiopian citizens elect them by direct vote.

Ethiopia's judicial system has two types of courts—state and federal. State courts handle cases that are of consequence only to a particular state. Federal courts hear cases that are important to the entire country. The Federal Supreme Court has final authority. Its judges are nominated by the prime minister, and they must meet approval by the House of People's Representatives.

The Ministry of Foreign Affairs manages the country's relationships with other nations. Ethiopia has been active in world politics since the end of World War II. In 1963, Emperor Haile Selassie played a key role in founding the Organization of African Unity (OAU), headquartered in Addis Ababa. A larger organization, the African Union, replaced the OAU in 2002. It helps its 53 member nations share information and resolve disputes.

During the border war with Eritrea (1998–2000), the Ethiopian National Defense Force reached a high of 350,000 soldiers. Since 2000, the army has steadily shrunk to its current level of about 200,000 soldiers. Ethiopia has only a tiny air force and, because it is a landlocked nation, no navy. Regardless, it still has one of the largest militaries in Africa. The United States provides training in such areas as military medicine and peacekeeping, as well as financial aid for counter-terrorism efforts.

POLITICAL ISSUES

Corruption is far less of a problem in Ethiopia than in some other African nations. Harsh laws are designed to punish corrupt government officials. Further, few people consider bribery and other forms of dishonesty to be acceptable practice in Ethiopia's deeply religious culture. In 2001, the government bolstered its laws with an anti-corruption commission to aggressively investigate any suspicious transactions. Although the commission's findings led to the arrests of numerous public officials and private businessmen, international observers were uncertain whether the arrests were legitimate or politically motivated.

Though not nearly as harsh and oppressive as the Derg had been, the current administration continues to draw criticism from human rights groups for its responses to domestic crises. In April 2001, student demonstrations in Addis Ababa turned deadly when police opened fire. The students had been peacefully protesting when some of the crowd began looting and vandalizing property. When the scene deteriorated into a riot, police fired into the mob and killed 41 people. While no one questioned the need to maintain public order, some groups felt that the police response was exceedingly violent.

The government has also been criticized for using the death penalty. International human rights groups have accused the Ethiopian government of executing more than 50 people over the past decade, either by firing squad or hanging. Most were former members of the Mengistu regime who had

Ethiopian soldiers march during an event in Fitche. Ethiopia's army is one of the largest in Africa.

been convicted of crimes against humanity. Approximately 6,000 other prisoners still await trial for their role in the Red Terror. Their decade-long imprisonment without a trial has prompted further censure by human rights organizations.

Events in recent years have further raised the issue of how much the government uses excessive force. Government troops were implicated in ethnic violence that began in December 2003 and continued into January. The series of incidents began when a United Nations vehicle was ambushed in the western region of Gambela and its eight occupants were murdered. Local residents blamed the killings on a nearby tribe called the Anyuak. Ethnic tension had already existed between the Anyuak and other groups, and the ambush sparked a retaliation that was even deadlier. A day after the ambush, in the regional capital of Gambela, a mob wielding axes, hatchets, and knives killed somewhere between 57 and 93 Anyuaks, according to conflicting reports. Some reports claimed that government troops reportedly stood by during the attack, and others said that they even played an active role in the murders. Afterward, roughly 5,000 Anyuaks fled across the border, seeking safety in Sudan and reporting to U.N. officials that Ethiopian soldiers had harassed and threatened them.

The Ethiopian Human Rights Council, an independent non-political organization, blames the Gambela incident and others like it on government policy. The council asserts that it was a mistake to establish states based on ethnic lines. Doing so has only allowed larger ethnic groups to consolidate power in each region and discriminate against minorities, according to the council. Intense debate continues to surround the issue.

Freedom of speech is another contentious issue for Ethiopians. The nation has a single television station, ETV, which the government runs. In 1999, a federal broadcasting authority was created to review applications for privately owned television stations, but to date no broadcasting licenses have been issued. Applicants claim that the delay is intentional and yet another example of how the government maintains its rigid control.

POLITICAL PARTIES

Ethiopia's first political parties were founded in the early 1960s during the rule of Emperor Haile Selassie. The goal of each party varied, but most had in common their opposition to the imperial government. Through their efforts, the parties unwittingly assisted in Mengistu and the Derg's rise to power. Among these groups was the Eritrean People's Liberation Front (EPLF).

New parties appeared in the 1970s to counter the Mengistu regime and fight for democracy. The Tigrayan People's Liberation Front (TPLF) joined forces with the EPLF and together they gained control of the country's north. In 1987, the TPLF created a coalition of like-minded parties in the south called the Ethiopian People's Revolutionary Democratic Front (EPRDF). The EPRDF coalition eventually swept Mengistu from power in 1991, and the EPRDF still controls the government today, despite mounting opposition from the Ogaden National Liberation Front.

With the country's first taste of democracy in the 1990s came dozens of new political parties. These organizations are continually forging new alliances, breaking into splinter groups, and renaming themselves. Even long-established parties within the EPRDF are not immune from turmoil. In 2001, the TPLF underwent an internal split due to discontent among its members.

For many Ethiopians, national politics is merely a game for which they have little time or patience. They are too busy coping with fighting poverty to worry about elections. With the country's literacy rate less than 43 percent, many people lack the means to stay up-to-date on the issues.

A handful of Ethiopian civic groups are dedicated to changing the voters' situation. These organizations hold workshops throughout the country to teach Ethiopians about their rights and responsibilities as citizens of a democracy. The civic education movement has earned praise from elected officials as well as international observers.

Agriculture is Ethiopia's main source of employment and income. (Opposite) A farmer guides his plow through the rocky soil of the Ethiopian highlands, near the Blue Nile. His fields will produce teff, the grain used for making *injera*, a traditional Ethiopian bread. (Right) Bundles of logs tied together in a lumberyard. Ethiopia is among the world's top lumber-producing nations.

4 An Economy in Transition

ETHIOPIA IS A NATION of farmers. At least 85 percent of the nation's work-force is engaged in agricultural activities. Many of these farmers are peasants cultivating small plots of land merely to survive; thus, their work generates little cash growth. Agriculture is frequently hampered by the north's erratic weather patterns. Drought adversely impacts the livelihoods of farmers as well as the profits of agricultural firms.

Ethiopia's employment and wage figures reveal a struggling economy: the nation's unemployment rate is estimated to be 40 percent; at least 45 per-cent of the population lives in poverty; and the *gross national income (GNI) per capita* is an astonishingly low $930. Government programs to heal the ailing economy are moving at a painfully slow pace.

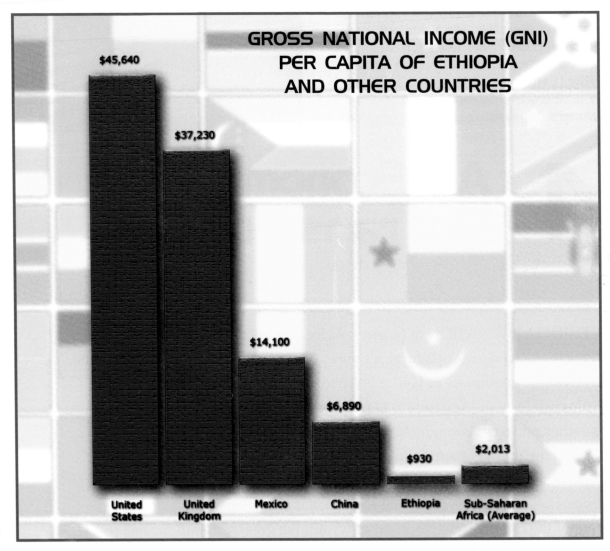

GROSS NATIONAL INCOME (GNI) PER CAPITA OF ETHIOPIA AND OTHER COUNTRIES

United States	$45,640
United Kingdom	$37,230
Mexico	$14,100
China	$6,890
Ethiopia	$930
Sub-Saharan Africa (Average)	$2,013

Gross national income per capita is the total value of all goods and services produced domestically in a year, supplemented by income received from abroad, divided by midyear population. The above figures take into account fluctuations in currency exchange rates and differences in inflation rates across global economies, so that an international dollar has the same purchasing power as a U.S. dollar has in the United States. Source: World Bank, 2011.

Although the Mengistu regime was ousted in 1991, Ethiopia's economy has not completely made the transition from the old socialist system. The government still owns most of the country's industries and essentially manages the economy. Prime Minister Meles Zenawi has stressed a program of *privatization*, in which the government sells off its interests to private companies.

Privatization will lead to a free market economy, in which business professionals will make the major financial decisions instead of government officials. The international community has encouraged and assisted the Ethiopian government in making this transition; however, it has been slow. Many government employees are resisting the change out of fear that private ownership will lead to layoffs. The Ethiopian Privatization Agency (EPA) is responsible for selling government companies. By the end of 2003, the EPA had sold more than 200 businesses, most of which were small shops, hotels, and restaurants. It is currently in the process of selling 117 more companies, including garment factories, textile mills, and food processing plants. Although some transitions have been made, the Ethiopian government will continue to regulate most of the nation's economy for some time to come.

Land reform is an essential element of privatization that has yet to be addressed. By law, all land in Ethiopia is owned by the government. Individuals are permitted to live on and farm the land, usually in small plots, but they cannot own it. Further, these plots of land become smaller as the population grows. In the most densely populated regions, an average plot is barely large enough to feed a single family.

IMPORTS AND EXPORTS

The combination of a struggling economy and explosive population growth require Ethiopia to import much more than it exports. In 2010, the country had a *trade deficit* of approximately $5 billion. The Ethiopian Mines and Energy Ministry announced in 2001 that it found deposits of oil, though it has not concluded how much exists. In 2005, a Chinese petroleum company began drilling an exploratory oil well in the Gambella basin, and additional mining efforts are underway elsewhere in the country. For now, however, Ethiopia's largest import remains petroleum, purchased from the Middle East. Other imports include cars, aircraft, construction vehicles, medicine, and agricultural equipment.

Coffee is easily Ethiopia's most important export, accounting for nearly half of the country's annual foreign revenue. In 1998, coffee exports reached an all-time high, as over 120,000 tons of high-quality arabica coffee were shipped with a value of $420 million. Since then, coffee production has slipped due to drought and a reduction in world demand. Germany, Japan, and Saudi Arabia are the biggest consumers of Ethiopian coffee. Together, those nations purchase nearly two-thirds of Ethiopia's coffee exports.

Reduced demand for coffee has forced the country to seek out new agricultural products. Over the past several years, Ethiopia has boosted production of tea, cotton, and sugar cane. Other exports include sesame seeds, spices, live animals, honey, and beeswax.

Leather is the country's second-largest export. Ethiopia has the largest concentration of livestock in Africa, which stands at about 75 million sheep, cattle, and goats. Leather products represent 13 percent of the country's total export value. The percentage could be higher if Ethiopians did not require so much of their livestock for food.

Another significant export in Ethiopia is a plant called *khat*. When chewed, the bitter-tasting khat stem makes the user feel alert and exhilarated. Because it is an addictive stimulant, khat is illegal in many parts of the world but is quite popular in East Africa. The plant makes a good crop for Ethiopian farmers because it grows in harsh conditions and requires little

THE ECONOMY OF ETHIOPIA

Gross domestic product (GDP*): $86.12 billion

Inflation: 7%

Natural Resources: small reserves of gold, platinum, copper, potash, natural gas, hydropower

Agriculture (42.9% of GDP): cereals, pulses, coffee, oilseed, sugarcane, potatoes, khat, hides, cattle, sheep, goats, fish

Industry (13.7% of GDP): food processing, beverages, textiles, chemicals, metals processing, cement

Services (43.4% of GDP): government, other

Economic Growth Rate: 8%

Foreign Trade:
Exports–$1.729 billion: coffee, khat, gold, leather products, live animals, oilseeds
Imports–$7.517 billion: food and live animals, petroleum and petroleum products, chemicals, machinery, motor vehicles, cereals, textiles

Currency Exchange Rate: U.S. $1 = 16.92 Ethiopian birrs (2011)

*GDP, or gross domestic product, is the total value of goods and services produced in a country annually.
All figures are 2010 estimates unless otherwise indicated.
Sources: CIA World Factbook, 2011

Khat, a mild narcotic, is a popular Ethiopian export even though it is illegal in many parts of the world.

care. Djibouti and Somalia purchase most of Ethiopia's khat export.

Despite its popularity, khat is harmful to the nation's populace and its economy. The drug has been shown to have damaging side effects, such as lethargy and insomnia, and in some people it can trigger violence. Khat is often sold and transported secretly, thus depriving the country of tax revenue. But even legal sales of khat bring farmers far more money than they receive for coffee. While an Ethiopian farmer might earn 15 cents for a pound of coffee, he can earn 10 times that much for a pound of khat.

Ethiopia trades with all of its immediate neighbors except for Eritrea. Other major trading partners are Saudi Arabia, the United Kingdom, China, Germany, Italy, India, and Japan. Since Ethiopia is a landlocked nation, and the border dispute between Ethiopia and Eritrea ended the countries' trade agreements, all imports and exports flow through the port of Djibouti.

Each year Ethiopia imports about $60 million of American goods, and a number of U.S. companies, including Boeing, Mobil Oil, and Coca-Cola, operate facilities in the country. In return, the United States purchases roughly 7 percent of Ethiopia's coffee exports and other items for a total of about $30 million. The U.S. government also makes significant donations to ease

Ethiopia's frequent resource crises. When the country was struck once again by famine in 2002, the United States contributed $475 million of food aid.

ECONOMIC CHALLENGES

Boosting foreign investment is a primary goal of the Ethiopian government. However, most foreign companies consider Ethiopia an inhospitable business environment. Government rules and regulations require much paperwork. Though the labor force is educated, it lacks highly skilled workers. Finally, basic infrastructure, such as roads and phone networks, are either in bad condition or in some places nonexistent.

With considerable aid from the global community, Ethiopia is addressing these problems. International financial agencies, such as the World Bank and the African Development Bank, have provided Ethiopia with billions of dollars in grants and loans since the mid-1990s. As a result, the country has implemented a long-term development program to establish economic growth and stability.

The first phase of this endeavor was the Road Sector Development Program, which ran from 1997-2010. Before the project began, Ethiopia had the lowest ratio in the world of road mileage per person. Now, both its major highways and community roads are greatly improved, which helps everyone conduct their business more efficiently.

The country's communications network has also been targeted for improvement. Presently, telephone service is very expensive and of poor quality, particularly outside the major cities. For years, cell phone service was available only in Addis Ababa, , but in recent years it has been expanded to include most major population centers. Internet service has also been established to a limited extent (primarily in Internet cafes), but speeds remain quite slow and less than 1 percent of the populace has access.

Ethiopia has the natural resources to generate huge volumes of hydroelectric (water-driven) energy and geothermal (steam-driven) energy. By taking advantage of this potential, Ethiopia would reduce its dependence on foreign oil and even export some of its own energy. Such developments might someday erase Ethiopia's annual trade deficit and perhaps even result in a trade surplus. At present, the government is concentrating on expanding hydroelectricity production. Several new power plants are under construction.

Tourism is another underdeveloped industry in Ethiopia. East Africa boasts exotic wildlife and is celebrated as the birthplace of the human species. Prehistoric artifacts and skeletons of early humans are on display at the National Museum in Addis Ababa and other museums in East Africa. Ethiopia's historical significance as a home to ancient civilizations is apparent through its countless stone churches and shrines. However, while other African nations like Kenya and South Africa generate hundreds of millions of dollars each year in tourism revenue, Ethiopia remains virtually unknown as a tourist destination. Officials hope that as the country's infrastructure needs are met, an increase in tourism will follow. At least one vital component for tourism is already in place: air travel. The nation's air carrier, Ethiopian Airlines, is widely regarded by aviation experts as the best in Africa. In addition to having numerous local routes, the airline flies to Europe, Asia, and the United States.

The Ethiopian government has long been dependent on foreign assis-

A young woman sick with AIDS lies in her bed at the Mother Teresa Home for Women and Children with AIDS in Addis Ababa. The people who die of the disease are generally of working age, and this has had a devastating impact on Ethiopia's economy.

tance to meet its financial obligations. Each year, the government must borrow hundreds of millions of dollars. International lenders have attempted to assist Ethiopia by rescheduling debt payments and, in some cases, canceling repayment altogether. Regardless, the government continues to borrow and the massive debt burden pushes the country deeper into poverty. In 2010, Ethiopia's foreign debt exceeded $4 billion.

Government officials argue that humanitarian crises, such as famine and widespread poverty, have compelled them to borrow so heavily. But economists believe that these problems have been worsened by government mismanagement and that the resistance to privatization has stifled economic growth. The government's refusal to implement land reform has discouraged farmers from investing in irrigation systems and other modern technologies. Most experts believe that until Ethiopia's government modernizes it policies, economic stability will never be achieved.

(Opposite) A Falasha, or Ethiopian Jew, shows off a souvenir for tourists in the village of Welek. (Right) Ethiopian Christians believe a biblical object called the Ark of the Covenant is located in this chapel in Aksum. The Ark is only taken out once a year, and may only be seen uncovered by an appointed guardian.

5 Diversity and Tradition

ETHIOPIA IS HOME TO one of the most diverse populations in the world. In East Africa, language is the characteristic most often used to distinguish ethnic groups. That there are 83 distinct languages spoken in Ethiopia, with more than 200 dialects, clearly demonstrates the diversity of the Ethiopian people.

The most populous ethnic group is the Oromo, who account for roughly 35 percent of the country's 90 million people. They live primarily in central and southern Ethiopia, in the state of Oromia. Farming and cattle-raising are Oromo traditions that span many centuries and generations. In fact, more than half of Ethiopia's agricultural products come from Oromia.

The Amhara and the Tigre make up Ethiopia's second-largest ethnic group. Though they share a common cultural and religious history as predominantly Coptic Christians, these two groups consider themselves very

THE PEOPLE OF ETHIOPIA

Population: 90,873,739 (July 2011 est.)

Ethnic Groups: Oromo 34.5%, Amara 26.9%, Somalie 6.2%, Tigraway 6.1%, Sidama 4%, Guragie 2.5%, Welaita 2.3%, Hadiya 1.7%, Affar 1.7%, Gamo 1.5%, Gedeo 1.3%, other 11.3% (2007 Census)

Age structure:
0–14 years: 46.3%
15–64 years: 51%
65 years and over: 2.7%

Population growth rate: 3.194%

Birth rate: 42.99 births/1,000 population

Infant mortality rate: 77.12 deaths/1,000 live births

Death rate: 11.04 deaths/1,000 population

Total fertility rate: 6.02 children born/woman

Life expectancy at birth:
total population: 56.19 years
male: 53.64 years
female: 58.81 years

Religion: Orthodox 43.5%, Muslim 33.9%, Protestant 18.6%, traditional 2.6%, Catholic 0.7%, other 0.7% (2007 Census)

Languages: Amharic, Tigrinya, Oromigna, Guaragigna, Somali, Arabic, other local languages, English (major foreign language taught in schools)

Literacy: 42.7% (2003 est.)

All figures are 2011 estimates unless otherwise indicated.
Source: Adapted from CIA World Factbook, 2011.

different and have often been at odds with each other. Residing in a large region to the north, the Amharas and Tigreans represent 33 percent of the nation's population. They are the descendants of the Aksum Empire and, like the Oromo, they rely heavily on agriculture for their livelihood. However, because Tigrean farmers reside in the far north, they are usually among the first victims of Ethiopia's many droughts.

Smaller ethnic groups include the Sidamo, who account for 9 percent of the population, and the Shankella and the Somali, who each account for 6 percent of the population. The Sidamo are the largest of 45 ethnic groups living in the state called Southern Nations, Nationalities and Peoples. The Shankella live in the country's west, along the border with Sudan, while the Somali live to the east. Both of these regions are extremely hot and undeveloped.

RELIGION

Despite all their ethnic differences, Ethiopians do share several traits and traditions. The most prominent of these is a deep devotion to religion. Over 60 percent of the population practices one of three denominations of Christianity (Egyptian Orthodox, Protestant, or Catholic), and another 34 percent are Muslim. The remaining minority represent a wide variety of native and imported beliefs.

The Ethiopian Orthodox Church is different in many ways from most of the world's churches. For many centuries after the religion was introduced, Ethiopian Christians remained isolated in the highlands, while Muslims occupied the surrounding lowlands. During this period of isolation, the Christians adopted some unique ceremonies and practices. Many of the rituals are rooted in Ethiopian legend, which is centered on the story of the Queen of Sheba and the Israelite King Solomon.

According to the legend, the Queen of Sheba traveled to Israel in the 10th century B.C. to honor King Solomon. Originally from the northern town of Aksum, she reigned over Ethiopia and southern Arabia. The two rulers fell in love, and shortly after returning to Ethiopia the queen gave birth to Solomon's

A Christian deacon attends a Timkat festival in Gonder. Observed in January, Timkat is the most important Ethiopian holiday. During this festival people dance, sing, and feast as each church's replica of the Ark of the Covenant is placed on display to celebrate the baptism of Christ.

son, whom she named Menelik. When he was 22 years old, Menelik went to Jerusalem to meet his father. While he was there he saw the Ark of the Covenant, a holy wooden chest believed to hold the Ten Commandments, and dreamed that God wanted him to take it back to Ethiopia.

The legend states Solomon was enraged to learn that Menelik took this precious religious artifact. He set out with his army to follow Menelik and retrieve the ark. During the journey, however, Solomon had his own dream confirming Menelik's vision. He returned to Jerusalem without the Ark, and it is believed to have remained in Aksum ever since.

The legend of the Ark has never been proven. The artifact, which is said to be stored in a closely guarded chapel, cannot be viewed by anyone but a special caretaker. Religious scholars outside Ethiopia remain highly skeptical that it is the actual Ark of the Covenant, though Ethiopian Christians fully believe in the legend. Every church in the country has a replica ark that is handled with the utmost reverence. In 2002, a 400-year-old replica that had been plundered by British troops in 1868 was returned to Ethiopia. Thousands of worshipers turned out in Addis Ababa to see the relic arrive by plane.

Ethiopian Christians celebrate an abundance of holidays, including 150 days of the year that honor various saints. The most important holiday is Timkat on January 19, which celebrates the baptism of Christ. This day holds far more meaning for Ethiopian Christians than any other holiday, including Christmas. On Timkat, each church's replica ark is carried to the nearest body of water. After prayers, the water is blessed and then splashed on the congregation. Afterward, the ark is carried back to the church amid singing and dancing.

Islam is the country's fastest-growing religion. Ethiopia's Muslim population was once limited to the lowlands, particularly in the east and south. Now Muslims live in all parts of the country, and mosques can be found throughout the highlands.

The beliefs of Ethiopian Muslims most closely resemble that of Islam's Sunni sect. However, just as with the Christian faith, traditional Islam has undergone some unique changes in Ethiopia. Specifically, it has split into many local branches and orders. Ethiopian worshipers place great importance on their particular branch's founder, who is usually considered a saint. Muslims residing in Ethiopia's cities are more likely to follow standard Islamic tradition than those living in rural areas.

Ethiopia has a small Jewish population. They are known as Falashas, and their numbers are constantly shrinking. Since the 1980s, the Israeli government has voiced concern over the conditions of Ethiopian Jews and has encouraged their immigration. On several occasions, it went as far as to send passenger jets to airlift the Falashas out of Ethiopia. Since the communities of most Ethiopian Jews are located in the drought-plagued northern regions, they have gladly accepted this offer of a new life. By early 2004, only 20,000 Falashas remained in Ethiopia and plans were underway to transport them to Israel as well.

CUSTOMS AND TRADITIONS

The wide variety of ethnic backgrounds and religious beliefs has fostered the development of countless local customs and traditions. Yet there are also practices that can be found almost universally throughout the country. An intriguing example is the calendar that Ethiopians follow. Beginning in 1582, much of the world's population started following the Gregorian calendar, which is still in use today. Ethiopia decided to remain with the Julian calendar, established by Roman emperor Julius Caesar, and still follows it today. The difference in perspective means that Ethiopia follows a calendar over eight years behind most other nations. In other words, when it was the year 2004 for the rest of the world, it was only 1996 in Ethiopia. To avoid confusion, most Ethiopian companies engaged in international business use the Gregorian calendar.

According to Ethiopian custom, it is proper to address a person by first name only. This is true whether the person is a friend or a stranger. As a show of respect, when speaking with a teacher or other person of authority an Ethiopian will place a title before the first name. The title *Ato* is used for a man, *Weizero* for a married woman, and *Weizerit* for a single woman. For example, an Ethiopian would address the current prime minister, Meles Zenawi, as Ato Meles.

For Ethiopians, the act of eating a meal together has special meaning. They believe that dining together fosters friendship and strengthens family bonds. The traditional Ethiopian dinner is a lengthy affair that includes several rituals. It begins when the guests are seated around a low table that resembles a woven basket. The host walks around the table with a clay water jug and pours water over each person's hands.

The national dish is a spicy stew called *wot*. It is served with a sour flatbread known as *injera*. People will dip the *injera* in the peppery *wot* sauce, or use it to scoop up pieces of chicken, beef, and vegetables. Before eating begins, the head of the household tears a piece of *injera* for each guest. After the meal, fresh honey is sometimes served as a dessert. The coffee ceremony then begins.

Ethiopians claim that coffee originated in their country. According to legend, Ethiopian monks began chewing on raw coffee beans over a thousand years ago to keep them alert during long prayer sessions. By the 13th

Two men prepare the dough for *injera*, or Ethiopian bread, in the town of Debre Libanos. The bread is usually eaten with a sauce made from chick-peas.

century, coffee beans were being roasted and used to brew the drink that is so popular today.

The lady of the household typically conducts the coffee ceremony. She begins by spreading fresh grass clippings and other aromatic plants in one corner of the room. She then takes a seat next to the wood stove and roasts the coffee beans in a pan. When roasting is completed, she takes the pan around so that each guest may enjoy the smell of the freshly cooked beans.

Afterward, the woman disappears into the kitchen to grind the beans and brew the coffee, then she emerges with a clay pot and small cups to serve the guests. Up to three pots may be brewed from the same coffee grounds. The third pot, which is the weakest, is for children.

A traditional dinner usually requires formal dress. Clothing styles vary widely between ethnic groups, and in recent years Western clothes have become popular. The color white is always considered fashionable among Ethiopians, regardless of style. Women wear white cotton robes and dresses and men wear loose-fitting tunics and pants. White outfits are frequently adorned with embroidered borders, which once only had religious patterns but now may contain a variety of themes, such as flowers and animals.

In the highlands, clothing is made of heavier material to provide warmth on cool evenings. Lowland clothing is sewn from thin cotton, and in these regions it is not uncommon for both men and women to go bare-chested. Jewelry such as necklaces, earrings, anklets, and hair ornaments are worn by virtually everyone. These items are made of gold, silver, ivory, and beads. Many people also carry decorative umbrellas as protection from the sun's harsh rays. Traditional costumes are typically worn during festivals and holidays, such as on the anniversary of the Battle of Adwa when men dress as traditional Ethiopian warriors.

(Opposite) The ruins of a castle in Gonder, once the most wealthy and populous city in East Africa. Gonder was the capital of Ethiopia from 1635 to 1867. (Right) A busy market in Addis Ababa, Ethiopia's current capital and one of Africa's largest population centers.

6 Villages, Towns, and Cities

MOST ETHIOPIANS LIVE in small rural communities. Only 3.1 million, or slightly less than 5 percent of the population, inhabit Ethiopia's major cities. The remaining 95 percent reside in small towns or rustic farming villages, some of which are located in very remote areas.

Lifestyles in these communities vary depending on locale and ethnic makeup. Oromo villages, for example, have a unique system of leadership. Only men between the ages of 24 and 32 may sit on the local governing council. Once a councilman turns 32, he must give up his seat to a younger man.

The economy of an Oromo village revolves around raising cattle. A family's status within the community is based on the number of cattle owned. In fact, a man who builds his herd to more than a thousand head of cattle is honored with a crown.

In contrast, the tiny minority of Dorze people in southern Ethiopia relies on weaving as a means of income. Hand-spun cotton cloth produced by Dorze weavers is renowned as the finest in the country. Dorze homes are tall, pear-shaped structures made entirely of bamboo. When a house begins to rot or become infested with termites, the entire community pitches in to help. Repairs are made to the damaged bamboo, then the entire house is lifted and carried to a new location.

Open-air markets and bazaars serve as the primary means of interaction between rural communities. Markets are situated along the roads between villages, and they are coordinated so that one is open every day of the week. Ethiopians go to the markets not only to acquire goods and supplies, but also to exchange news and gossip. A variety of handmade crafts are also sold at the markets. Since the Ethiopian tourist industry is virtually nonexistent, tradesmen make crafts with fellow Ethiopians in mind. Such items, which are usually more functional than ornamental, include woven hats and baskets, clay cooking utensils, clothing, toys, and religious objects.

Ethiopia's city-dwellers do their shopping in malls and traditional stores. However, unlike other African nations, there are relatively few Western retail shops in Ethiopia. Only Addis Ababa has a significant presence of foreign-owned department stores, hotels, and restaurants.

ADDIS ABABA

In 1887, Emperor Menelik II decided to move the empire's capital from Amhara in the north toward the center of the country. His wife chose the name Addis Ababa for the new city, which means "new flower." The first few years in the highland city were difficult. There was a shortage of trees in the region, and firewood had to be transported from great distances.

At one point, the emperor was contemplating abandoning the city when an advisor made a valuable suggestion. He had noticed a thriving cluster of imported Eucalyptus trees, and recommended that large quantities of the tree be planted throughout Addis Ababa. The emperor ordered it done, and soon the city's firewood problem was solved.

Addis Ababa developed into a truly modern city during the early decades of the 20th century. It became home to Ethiopia's first advanced facilities, including a hospital, a bank, and a printing press. Once it was connected by rail with the port of Djibouti in 1915, the city grew even more rapidly. Colleges, hotels, and government buildings were constructed, as well as the nation's first airport.

During its relatively short history, Addis Ababa has fallen into turmoil on three separate occasions. The Italian invasion and occupation of the late 1930s and early 1940s halted the city's growth and forced many institutions to close. Similar disruptions occurred with the overthrow of Emperor Haile Selassie in 1974 and the successful rebellion against the Mengistu regime in 1991. In each crisis, the city emerged from the chaos and experienced a new stage of expansion.

Today, Addis Ababa is one of the largest population centers in Africa (estimated population: 3.4 million) and is considered the continent's diplomatic hub. In addition to holding the headquarters of the African Union, it also hosts the United Nations Economic Commission for Africa and over 70 embassies.

The majority of the city's residents work either for one of these institutions or for the Ethiopian government in some capacity.

Addis Ababa is also Ethiopia's cultural center. The National Museum of Ethiopia has been heralded as the best museum of its kind in Africa. Among other priceless artifacts, it houses the ancient remains of a *hominid* affectionately called Lucy. Estimated to be 3.5 million years old, Lucy was once considered the earliest known ancestor of humankind. Portions of her skeleton were discovered in northern Ethiopia in 1974.

The National Theater in downtown Addis Ababa stages a variety of cultural events such as plays and concerts. Ethiopian folk music is known as *zefen*. It is performed with traditional instruments constructed of wood, animal hide, and horsehair strings. *Zefen* is often accompanied by a traditional dance known as *iskista*. Modern music, particularly jazz, is also popular and can be heard in many of the city's restaurants and nightclubs.

Addis Ababa Stadium routinely draws large crowds to see international soccer matches. In Ethiopia, as in most places outside North America, soccer is known as *football*. Long-distance running is the second most popular sport in Ethiopia, and professional runners train in the city's streets. At an elevation of 7,800 feet (2,400 meters), Addis Ababa is an ideal place for runners to build up their stamina.

OTHER CITIES

With an estimated population of 600,000, Dire Dawa is the only other metropolis in Ethiopia large enough to be a self-governing city-state. It is the nation's most important industrial center, and lies roughly halfway along the

Addis Ababa–Djibouti railroad. It was this prime location next to the railroad that compelled settlers to found the city in 1902.

The city is divided in half by the Dachata River. The Dachata is actually just a damp riverbed for most of the year, but during rainy seasons it can become a raging torrent. Dire Dawa's main industries are cement and textiles. The city has grown in both population and strategic importance in recent years. The border war with Eritrea left Djibouti as Ethiopia's only accessible seaport. Consequently, Dire Dawa has become a staging area for international trade.

Nearby Harer is also a major population center, with 147,000 residents. Founded as early as the 10th century, it is one of East Africa's oldest cities. As a trading center prized by rival kings and sultans, the city was the site of many battles. In the 1560s, a huge stone wall was built around the city for protection from invaders. The wall still stands today, but Harer has spread far beyond its confines.

The farms surrounding the city produce high-quality coffee and khat, but with more than 90 mosques, Harer is best known as an Islamic holy city. For several centuries, Christians were not permitted within its walls. Today, they are welcome in the city but the residents of the old, walled section are still predominantly Muslim.

Other major cities in Ethiopia include Dese, Nazret, and Bahir Dar. Nestled at the base of Mount Tossa in the north, Dese is an administrative post with modern office buildings. During the Italian invasion in 1935, it briefly served as Emperor Haile Selassie's headquarters before he was forced to flee.

Nazret takes its name from the biblical town of Nazareth. Located a

A view of the Great Mosque in Harer, a city in eastern Ethiopia. Arabs founded the city in the seventh century, and most of its inhabitants still follow Islam.

short distance southeast of Addis Ababa, Nazret is primarily agricultural with huge plantations for growing fruit and sugar cane. Sitting on the southern shores of Lake Tana, Bahir Dar is the capital of the state of Amhara. It is one of the fastest-growing cities in Ethiopia due to a small but thriving tourism industry. A nearby ethnic group called the Woyto sail Lake Tana in handmade canoes called *tankwas*. Despite being constructed only of papyrus and having an open back end, *tankwas* have been used to navigate the lake for countless Woyto generations.

North of Lake Tana is Ethiopia's former capital city of Gonder. Although Gonder has suffered a declining population in recent decades, its historical significance is undeniable. The city became Ethiopia's capital in 1632 and remained so for more than two centuries. During this period, Gonder became the most populous and wealthy city in East Africa, attracting traders and craftspeople from all over the region. Gonder's decline began in the late 19th century after Emperor Theodore II moved the capital to another location. Heavy fighting during World War II quickened the city's deterioration, yet many of Gonder's old castles and palaces still remain standing. They are a proud tribute to a golden era in Ethiopian history.

Few nations can claim to have a past as distinctive as Ethiopia's. It is an extensive history marked by conflict and suffering, but one that also includes many achievements and triumphs. In 1991, Ethiopians ended the darkest chapter in their history with the expulsion of the Mengistu regime. Since then they have taken the first steps toward building a free and prosperous society. Persistent obstacles such as famine and poverty continue to stand in their way, but Ethiopians have persistently coped with hardship. Through continued world support and insightful elected leaders, this misunderstood nation finally has an opportunity to rise above its problems.

A CALENDAR OF ETHIOPIAN FESTIVALS

Instead of following the Gregorian calendar, used in most of the world's countries, Ethiopians follow the Julian calendar. The following dates are listed as they appear in the Gregorian calendar and thus differ between 7 and 11 days from their Julian counterparts.

January

Celebrated on January 7, **Ethiopian Christmas** is a major Orthodox Christian holiday. It follows 43 days of fasting, during the season known as Advent. Christians break the fast by eating a chicken, lamb, or beef and traditional foods.

Christians celebrate the baptism of Jesus Christ on **Timkat**, January 19. It is the most important Christian holiday in Ethiopia. On the eve of Timkat, people gather to attend colorful processions and to eat a specially baked bread called *himbash*. Sheep are also slaughtered.

March

Held on March 2, the **Victory of Adwa** celebration commemorates the 1896 battle in which Ethiopian forces defeated Italian invaders.

April

On April 6, people celebrate **Patriots Victory Day** to honor those who fought against the Italian occupation of 1935–41.

May

In Ethiopia and many other countries of the world, **Labor Day**, May 1, honors the workers.

May 29, the **Downfall of the Derg**, commemorates the ouster of the Mengistu regime in 1991.

September

The **Ethiopian New Year**, or **Enkutatash**, falls on September 11 (or September 12 during a leap year). The day is also a religious holiday, commemorating Saint John the Baptist.

On September 28, **Meskel** is an Orthodox Christian holiday that remembers the finding of the True Cross. According to church tradition, the Roman empress and saint Helena found the buried cross on which Jesus Christ was crucified and gave pieces of it to various churches, including the Ethiopian Church.

Religious Observances

Ethiopia's Muslims and Christians observe a number of important holy days related to their religions. Some of these are on particular days each year, but many other major celebrations are held according to a lunar calendar, in which the months correspond to the phases of the moon. A lunar month is shorter than a typical month of the Western calendar. Therefore, the festival dates vary from year to year. Other celebrations are observed seasonally.

A very important month of the Muslim lunar calendar is the ninth month, **Ramadan**. This is a time of sacrifice for devout Muslims. Ethiopian Muslims celebrate **Eid al-Fitr** to mark the end of Ramadan. **Eid al-Adha** (Feast of Sacrifice) takes place in the last month of the Muslim calendar during the hajj period, when Muslims make a pilgrimage to Mecca. The holiday honors the prophet Abraham, who was willing to sacrifice his own son to Allah. Each of these holidays is celebrated with a feast. On Eid al-Adha, families traditionally eat a third of the feast and donate the rest to the poor.

The major Christian festivals on the lunar cycle involve the suffering and death of Jesus Christ. **Ash Wednesday** marks the start of a period of self-sacrifice called **Lent**, which lasts for 40 days. The final eight days of Lent are known as Holy Week. A number of important days are observed, including **Palm Sunday**, which commemorates Jesus' arrival in Jerusalem; **Holy Thursday**, which marks the night of the Last Supper; **Good Friday**, the day of Jesus' death on the cross; and **Fasika** (Easter Monday), which marks his resurrection. (In Western countries, Easter is typically celebrated on the day before.)

RECIPES

Injera (Flat Bread)

(Serves 4 to 6)
2 cups self-rising flour
4 cups water
1 tsp. baking powder
6 Tbsp. pancake mix

Directions:
1. Mix the flour and water together in a bowl; let stand overnight. Pour off any water that has risen to the top.
2. Combine flour mixture, baking powder, and pancake mix in blender. Blend on high until smooth, adding more water if necessary to make a thin batter.
3. Heat a 10-inch non-stick skillet over medium-high heat. Pour in 1/2 cup of the batter and immediately tilt the skillet to create a thin pancake. Cover and cook for about one minute.
4. Transfer to platter. Repeat with the remaining batter.

Doro Wot (Spicy Chicken Stew)

(Serves 8)
8 red onions, peeled and quartered
1 cup clarified butter
1 cup *berbere* spice mix (see recipe below)
1 1/2 cups water
8 chicken legs, skinned
4 skinless chicken breast halves, cut in half
5 cloves garlic, chopped
1 Tbsp. ground nutmeg
4 hard-cooked eggs, peeled and quartered

Directions:
1. Puree onions in food processor. Transfer onions to saucepan. Cook, stirring often, over medium heat, until onions are lightly browned and liquid from onions has evaporated.
2. Reduce heat to low. Stir in clarified butter, *berbere* mix, and 1 cup of the water. Cook 15 minutes.
3. Add chicken and remaining 1/2 cup water. Simmer for 30 minutes.
4. Stir in garlic and cook 10 minutes, then stir in nutmeg and cook 5 minutes.
5. Transfer to platter and garnish with eggs.

Berbere (Spice Mix)

(Makes 1 cup)
1/4 cup sweet paprika
1/4 cup ground red pepper
2 Tbsp. salt
2 Tbsp. garlic powder
1 Tbsp. ground allspice
1 Tbsp. ground cardamom pods

Directions:
1. Combine paprika, red pepper, salt, garlic powder, and allspice in a small bowl.
2. Heat a small, dry skillet over medium heat. Add cardamom pods and heat for about 3 minutes. Let cool.
3. Grind in spice grinder or clean coffee grinder. Add to spice mixture, stirring to mix well.

Kik Alicha (Yellow Split Pea Stew)

(Serves 6)
3 cups water plus 2 Tbsp.
1 cup dried yellow split peas
2 Tbsp. olive oil
1 small onion, chopped
2 cloves garlic, minced
1 small piece fresh ginger root, peeled and finely chopped
1/2 tsp. turmeric
1 tsp. salt

Directions:
1. Place 3 cups of the water and peas in a large saucepan. Heat over high heat until boiling. Reduce heat to medium. Cook for about 30 minutes.
2. Heat olive oil in a medium skillet over medium-high heat; cook onion for about 5 minutes. Add garlic, ginger, and turmeric. Cook 1 minute.
3. Add remaining 2 tablespoons of water. Cover and cook on low heat for 3 minutes.
4. Add mixture to cooked peas and stir in salt. Simmer until peas are very soft, about 30 minutes.

GLOSSARY

amoles—salt bricks, such as those mined in the Danakil Desert in northern Ethiopia.

arable—capable of being cultivated for growing crops.

Ato—a title for males, equivalent to *Mr.* in English.

Ge'ez—the written language of the Aksum Empire.

gross national income (GNI) per capita—the total value of all goods and sevices produced domestically in a year, supplemented by income received from abroad, divided by midyear population.

hominid—the family of primates that includes humans.

infrastructure—apparatus vital to economic activity, such as roads and communication networks.

iskista—traditional Ethiopian folk dance.

khat—a hardy plant that acts as a mild stimulant when chewed.

ky kebero—literally "red jackal," it is the world's most rarest canine species and native only to the Simien mountain range.

landlocked—closed in by land, with no direct access to a major body of water.

plateau—an elevated, flat tract of land.

privatization—the selling of state-owned businesses to private investors.

socialism—a political system in which the government owns all industries and institutions.

tankwas—handmade canoes built by the Woyto people near Lake Tana.

trade deficit—a negative balance in trade in which a nation's imports exceed its exports.

walia ibex—a nearly extinct species of mountain goat found only in the Simien mountain range.

Weizero—title for a married woman, equivalent to *Mrs.* in English.

Weizerit—title for a single woman, equivalent to *Miss* or *Ms.* in English.

woredas—local administrative districts.

zefen—traditional Ethiopian folk music.

PROJECT AND REPORT IDEAS

Maps and Posters

Draw a map that shows the geography of Ethiopia. It should include the following features: Ras Dejen, Lake Tana, the Ethiopian highlands, the Great Rift Valley, the Simien mountain range, and the Danakil Desert. Also include Ethiopia's capital, Addis Ababa, and its second-largest city, Dire Dawa.

Create a timeline of Ethiopian history. Begin your timeline with the Aksum Empire in the first century A.D. and end it with the famine of 2002. In between those time periods, mark what you feel are the 10 most important years in Ethiopian history. Identify the event(s) that made each year important. The chronology that appears on the following pages will help you with this project.

Gather pictures of animal species that are native only to Ethiopia. Include pictures of Ethiopia's endangered species, such as the Simien wolf, walia ibex, and mountain nyala. Pictures can be photocopied from encyclopedias, travel guides, and other books, or printed from the Internet. Make a poster using the pictures you gathered. Write the name of each species beneath its picture, and identify endangered species with a red star.

Reports

Read articles in newspapers, magazines, and on the Internet about Ethiopia's most recent famine. Write a two-page report about what you learned. Be sure to answer the following questions in your report: When did the famine begin? Has the famine ended or is it still going on? How many Ethiopians were impacted? Which countries or international organizations donated food and medicine to help Ethiopia?

In recent years, the border dispute with Eritrea has been a major issue in Ethiopia. Many countries around the world have criticized Ethiopia for refusing to accept an international committee's resolution to the disagreement. Find out the latest news on the border dispute. Look for articles in newspapers, current events magazines, and on the Internet. Either write a two-page report on your findings or give an oral presentation to your class.

Traditional Meal Presentation

Give an oral presentation about the food and customs of a traditional Ethiopian meal, including information on *wot, injera,* and coffee. Explain the customs of pouring water over guests' hands, tearing off a piece of *injera* for each guest, and the coffee ceremony, and the meanings they may have for the people who follow them. Find pictures or other visual aids that will help illustrate your presentation.

CHRONOLOGY

1st century A.D.	The Aksum Empire rises in northern Ethiopia.
ca. 750	The Aksum Empire declines and Ethiopia becomes isolated.
1270	Yekuno Amlak becomes emperor and leads Ethiopia out of its dark age.
1543	Portugal assists the highland Christians in defeating the lowland Muslims.
1869	Emperor Theodore II commits suicide while facing capture by British troops.
1889	A treaty dispute leads to war between Ethiopia and Italy.
1896	Ethiopian forces defeat Italian troops at the Battle of Adwa.
1930	Haile Selassie is crowned emperor.
1935	Italy invades and occupies Ethiopia.
1941	British forces liberate Ethiopia; Haile Selassie returns to power.
1960	A military coup against Haile Selassie is put down.
1973	A major famine sweeps the north, killing 200,000 people.
1974	Haile Selassie is overthrown by the military; a council of military officers known as the Derg, led by Colonel Mengistu Haile Mariam, takes control of the country.
1977	The Mengistu regime initiates a campaign of violence known as the Red Terror.
1985	Roughly one million people die in one of the worst famines in history.
1991	Rebel insurgents sweep Mengistu from power and establish a democracy.
1993	The northern province of Eritrea is granted independence.

1998	A border dispute between Ethiopia and Eritrea erupts into warfare.
2000	Hostilities cease but the border disagreement remains unresolved.
2002	Northern Ethiopia experiences another drought-induced famine.
2003–2004	Dozens of ethnic Anyuaks die in fighting that breaks out in December 2003 and lasts four more weeks; government troops are accused of participating in the attacks.
2005	The remains of ancient royal tombs are found underground near Axum; experts believe some of the tombs may still be intact.
2006	12-year trial of exiled former dictator Mengistu Haile Mariam ends with a conviction for genocide and a sentence of death. Mariam remains in Zimbabwe, where he was granted asylum in 1991.
2009	In January, Ethiopia withdraws its troops from Somalia, ending a two-year occupation of the conflict-torn nation.
2010	Ruling EPRDF party wins a large majority in contested parliamentary elections; the Ogaden National Liberation Front continues to wage violent uprisings against the government.
2011	Ethiopia suffers from a terrible drought, leading to widespread famine; in July, 4,200 Ethiopian peacekeepers are sent to the oil-rich Abyei territory to replace a U.N. force that had been operating in Sudan.
2012	The government works with foreign organizations to combat the effects of drought and famine.

FURTHER READING/INTERNET RESOURCES

Briggs, Philip. *Ethiopia: The Bradt Travel Guide, 5th edition.* Guilford, Conn.: The Globe Pequot Press, 2009.

Heinrichs, Ann. *Ethiopia* (Enchantment of the World Series). Danbury, Conn.: Children's Press, 2005.

Howard, Sarah. *Ethiopia – Culture Smart!* London: Kuperard, 2009.

Mockler, Anthony. *Haile Selassie's War.* New York: Interlink Publishing Group, 2002.

Munro-Hay, Stuart C. *Ethiopia, the Unknown Land: A Cultural and Historical Guide.* New York: I. B. Tauris Publishers, 2002.

Pankhurst, Richard. *The Ethiopians: A History.* Malden, Mass.: Blackwell Publishers, 2001.

Travel Information

http://www.state.gov/r/pa/ei/bgn/2859.htm
http://www.tourismethiopia.org/

History and Geography

http://www.ethiopianhistory.com/index.php
https://www.cia.gov/library/publications/the-world-factbook/geos/et.html
http://www.abyssiniacybergateway.net/ethiopia/history/pankhurst.html

Economic and Political Information

http://www.ethiopianembassy.org/
http://news.bbc.co.uk/2/hi/africa/country_profiles/1072164.stm

Culture and Festivals

http://www.selamta.net/
http://www.lonelyplanet.com/ethiopia

FOR MORE INFORMATION

Embassy of Ethiopia
3506 International Drive, NW
Washington, DC 20008
Tel: (202) 364-1200
Website: http://www.ethiopianembassy.org/

U.S. Embassy in Ethiopia
Entoto Street
P.O. Box 1014
Addis Ababa
Tel: 011-130-6000
Fax: 011-124-2401
Email: pasaddis@state.gov
Website: http://ethiopia.usembassy.gov/

U.S. Department of State
Bureau of Consular Affairs
2100 Pennsylvania Ave. NW, 4th Floor
Washington, DC 20037
Tel: (202) 736 9130

INDEX

Numbers in ***bold italic*** refer to captions.

CONTRIBUTORS

Professor Robert I. Rotberg is Director of the Program on Intrastate Conflict and Conflict Resolution at the Kennedy School, Harvard University, and President of the World Peace Foundation. He is the author of a number of books and articles on Africa, including *A Political History of Tropical Africa* and *Ending Autocracy, Enabling Democracy: The Tribulations of Southern Africa*.

Jim Corrigan has authored numerous newspaper and magazine articles, as well as several nonfiction books for students. A full-time freelance writer, Corrigan specializes in topics relating to history, travel, and ethnic studies. His books for young readers include *The Civil War in the West, Europeans and Native Americans*, and *Filipino Immigration*. He is a graduate of Penn State University and currently resides near Harrisburg, Pennsylvania.